TURNING POINTS IN U.S. HISTORY

CALIFORNIA GOLD RUSH

by Veronica B. Wilkins

pogo

Ideas for Parents and Teachers

Pogo Books let children practice reading informational text while introducing them to nonfiction features such as headings, labels, sidebars, maps, and diagrams, as well as a table of contents, glossary, and index.

Carefully leveled text with a strong photo match offers early fluent readers the support they need to succeed.

Before Reading

- "Walk" through the book and point out the various nonfiction features. Ask the student what purpose each feature serves.
- Look at the glossary together. Read and discuss the words.

Read the Book

- Have the child read the book independently.
- Invite him or her to list questions that arise from reading.

After Reading

- Discuss the child's questions. Talk about how he or she might find answers to those questions.
- Prompt the child to think more. Ask: Many people moved across the country during the California gold rush. Do you know of other times when many people moved to other parts of the country?

Pogo Books are published by Jump!
5357 Penn Avenue South
Minneapolis, MN 55419
www.jumplibrary.com

Library of Congress Cataloging-in-Publication Data

Names: Wilkins, Veronica B., 1994- author.
Title: California Gold Rush / Veronica B. Wilkins.
Description: Minneapolis, MN: Jump!, Inc., [2020]
Series: Turning points in U.S. history | Includes index.
Audience: Ages 7-10.
Identifiers: LCCN 2019020318 (print)
LCCN 2019021931 (ebook)
ISBN 9781645271314 (ebook)
ISBN 9781645271291 (hardcover : alk. paper)
ISBN 9781645271307 (pbk.)
Subjects: LCSH: California–Gold discoveries
Juvenile literature. | California–History–1846-1850
Juvenile literature.
Classification: LCC F865 (ebook)
LCC F865 .W67 2020 (print)
DDC 979.4/04–dc23
LC record available at https://lccn.loc.gov/2019020318

Editor: Susanne Bushman
Designer: Jenna Casura

Photo Credits: Science History Images/Alamy, cover; Spencer Weiner/Los Angeles Times/Getty, 1l; undefined undefined/iStock, 1r; Huntington Library/SuperStock, 3; Bettmann/Getty, 4l, 5; MPI/Getty, 4r; BLM Collection/Alamy, 6-7; De Agostini Picture L/Age Fotostock, 8-9; Apic/Getty, 10; Everett Historical/Shutterstock, 11, 14-15; Everett Collection Inc./Age Fotostock, 12-13; Lawrence & Houseworth/Library of Congress, 16; Frank and Frances Carpenter Collection/Library of Congress, 17; Joke van Eeghem/Shutterstock, 18-19; Sean Pavone/Shutterstock, 20-21; Africa Studio/Shutterstock, 23.

Printed in the United States of America at Corporate Graphics in North Mankato, Minnesota.

TABLE OF CONTENTS

CHAPTER 1

FINDING GOLD

On January 24, 1848, men were building a sawmill on a river near Coloma, California. James W. Marshall was one of these workers.

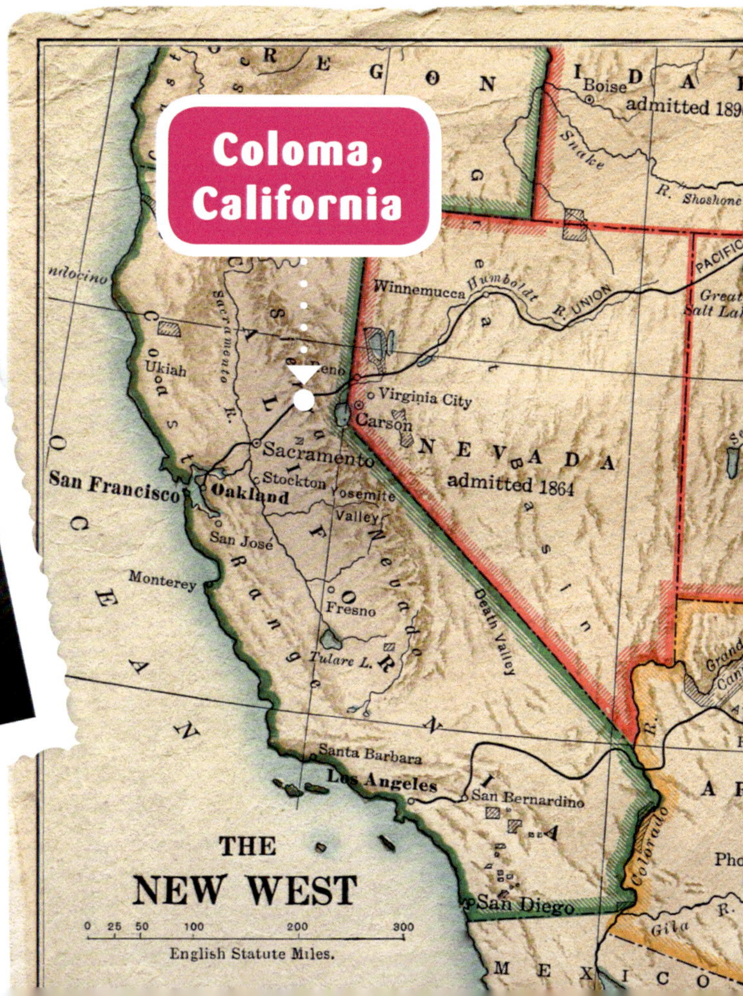

Marshall saw something shiny in the water. It was gold! He told his boss, John Sutter. Sutter asked the workers to keep the gold a secret. Why? It was worth a lot of money!

San Francisco,
1848

But the secret got out. A newspaper reported the story on March 15, 1848. Few readers believed it.

Then Sam Brannan told people in San Francisco. Why? He owned a store near the discovery. He wanted gold seekers to come to his store. His plan worked. Many came to search for gold. The California gold rush began.

CALIFORNIAN

BY B. R. BUCKELEW.

SAN FRANCISCO, MARCH 15, 1848

Gold Mine Found – In the newly made raceway of the Saw Mill recently erected by Captain Sutter, on the American Fork, gold has been found in considerable quantities. One person brought thirty dollars worth to New Helvetia, gathered

News of the gold continued to spread. Thousands of people came to California between 1848 and 1855. They hoped to get rich finding gold.

Before the gold rush, many Native American, Mexican, and Spanish people lived here. There were only a few white **settlers**.

DID YOU KNOW?

Nine days after the gold was found, the Mexican-American War (1846-1848) ended. The United States gained land. This land later became the states of California, Nevada, Utah, Arizona, and New Mexico.

CHAPTER 2

HUNTING FOR GOLD

Getting to California was hard. Why? People came in covered wagons. The journey west across North America was long. Mountains were hard to cross.

Sailing across the Pacific Ocean was easier. Miners came from countries like Peru, Chile, China, New Zealand, and Australia. Others sailed from the U.S. East Coast. Many ship crews left their ships in San Francisco to search for gold.

boomtown

About 80,000 men came to California in 1849. This is why people called them Forty Niners. Small towns became crowded **boomtowns**. Living in these towns could be dangerous. Why? They had few laws.

WHAT DO YOU THINK?

Many store owners were richer than gold miners! Why? Supplies were in **demand**. Store owners could charge a lot. Do you think this was fair? Why or why not?

Miners spent their days looking for gold. At first, they **panned** for it in rivers. But panning was slow. Rocker boxes sped up the process.

TAKE A LOOK!

Take a look at how rocker boxes worked!

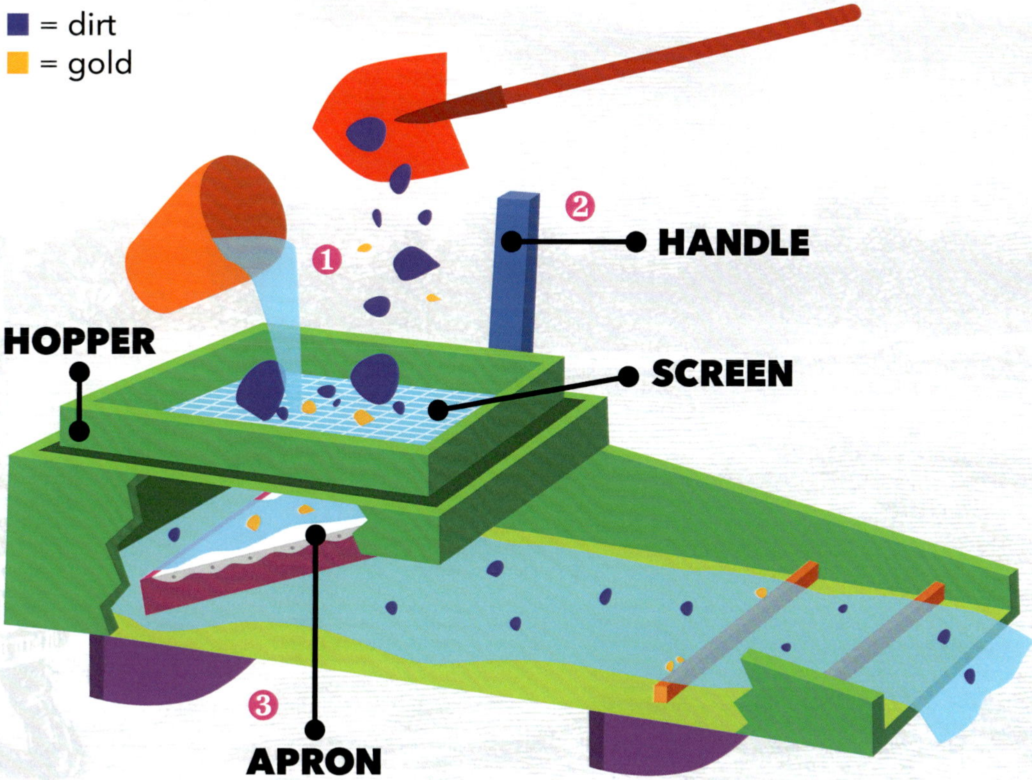

1. Water and dirt are poured into the hopper. A screen catches sticks and stones.
2. A miner rocks the box with the handle. This separates gold from dirt. Gold is heavier. It settles.
3. Dirt washes away. Gold is left on the apron. Miners collect it by hand.

CHAPTER 3

THE GOLD RUSH ENDS

There was only so much gold on Earth's surface. Miners found much of it. **Hydraulic mining** began in 1853. Miners sprayed water into mines. This helped find gold underground.

But hydraulic mining was bad for Earth. Mines left holes in the countryside. Rivers filled with dirt from mines. This made it hard for **crops** to grow.

By 1855, there was little gold left to be found on Earth's surface. Hydraulic mining needed fewer miners. Many miners left. Boomtowns were left empty. They became **ghost towns**.

ghost town

San Francisco

About 250,000 people came to California to find gold during the gold rush. Between 1847 and 1860, the state's **population** tripled. California would never be the same. It became home to people from around the world. San Francisco grew into a large city.

WHAT DO YOU THINK?

Many **foreign** miners faced **prejudice** from white miners. Some were even attacked! There was also a special tax for foreign miners. How do you think this felt?

QUICK FACTS & TOOLS

TIMELINE

JANUARY 24, 1848
James W. Marshall finds gold in a California creek.

FEBRUARY 2, 1848
The Treaty of Guadalupe Hidalgo ends the Mexican-American War. It gives the United States control of California.

MARCH 15, 1848
The Californian, a newspaper in San Francisco, reports the discovery of gold.

MAY 1848
Sam Brannan spreads news of the gold in San Francisco.

AUGUST 1848
A newspaper in New York reports the discovery of gold.

DECEMBER 5, 1848
President James Polk confirms the discovery of gold in California in his State of the Union Address.

SEPTEMBER 9, 1850
California becomes a state.

1853
Hydraulic mining is first used by Edward Matteson.

1860
California's population has tripled since the start of the gold rush.

GLOSSARY

boomtowns: Towns that experienced rapid growth due to sudden prosperity.

crops: Plants grown for food.

demand: Desire to buy or use something.

foreign: Of, having to do with, or coming from another country.

ghost towns: Deserted towns with few or no people living there.

hydraulic mining: Mining that is powered by liquid moving through pipes under pressure.

panned: Washed gravel in a pan or sieve to look for gold.

population: The total number of people who live in a place.

prejudice: An opinion that is formed about a person or a group of people before getting to know them.

sawmill: A place where people use machines to saw logs into lumber.

settlers: People who make homes or live in a new place.

INDEX

TO LEARN MORE

Finding more information is as easy as 1, 2, 3.

1. Go to www.factsurfer.com
2. Enter "Californiagoldrush" into the search box.
3. Choose your book to see a list of websites.

FACT SURFER